A Relaxation Book for Children Who Live With Anxiety

When My Worries Get Too Big!

Second Edition - Revised

Written and Illustrated by
Kari Dunn Buron

Foreword by Brenda Smith Myles, PhD

©2022 5 Point Scale Publishing
www.5pointscale.com

All rights reserved. No part of the material protected by this copyright notice may be reproduced or used in any form or by any means, electronic or mechanical, including photocopying, recording, or by any information storage and retrieval system, without the prior written permission of the copyright owner.

Buron, Kari Dunn.

When My Worries Get Too Big!: a relaxation book for children who live with anxiety/ written and illustrated by Kari Dunn Buron; foreword by Brenda Smith Myles -- 2nd Edition - Revised. 5 Point Scale Publishing ©2022.

ISBN: 978-1-7376715-6-5 (eBook)
        978-1-7376715-5-8 (Paperback)
Library of Congress Control Number 2021924669
Revision of the 2006 1st edition.
Summary: An illustrated children's book about coping with anxiety. This edition includes notes for parents and teachers.

1. Anxiety in children - - Treatment - - Juvenile literature. 2. Emotional Regulation in children - - Treatment - - Juvenile literature. 3. Resilience in children - - Treatment - - Juvenile Literature. 4. Children with autism - - Treatment - - Juvenile literature. 5. Explosive Behavior in children - - Treatment - - Juvenile literature.

Printed in the United States of America

This book is dedicated to anxious children everywhere.

Foreword

Children and youth who experience problems controlling their anxiety and behavior are complex because they have a multifaceted disability that manifests itself differently within each individual. In short, if you have seen one child with anxiety or behavior regulation problems, you have seen one child with these challenges. The next child you work or live with may look or act completely differently!

This unique individuality presents challenges to teachers, parents, and researchers attempting to develop interventions that consistently address the needs inherent in the exceptionality but are flexible enough to be used with many children. Partnered with this task is the need for interventions that can be implemented without an extensive time investment (because there is never enough time at home or at school!) and that can be used in both general and special education environments as well as in homes and communities. Not many interventions have been able to meet these demanding requirements.

Every once in a while an intervention comes across my desk that meets these criteria. When My Worries Get Too Big! is one such gift. This structured yet flexible, child and adult friendly intervention can be used in many environments. In this charming book, Kari Dunn Buron, whose years of experience with individuals with anxiety and behavior control problems truly make her an expert, has addressed some of the biggest challenges experienced by many of our children and youth — the inability to self-monitor stress, the rapid escalation from worry to meltdowns, and problems knowing how to relax or return to a state of calmness. Kari refers to these situations as "when my worries get too big." The term "worries" here refers to the quick escalation to meltdowns.

This book is intended to help children with anxiety and emotional control problems understand that sometimes their worries get too big and that they are not alone in this challenge. To make this more concrete, Kari rates the "bigness" of worries on a 5-point scale, with a rating of "1" meaning little or no stress and a rating of "5" referring to the stage when the worry is "way too big" and may result in a meltdown. She empowers children by telling them that they can fight back against the "bigness of their worries" and take control in trying to return to or remain in a calm state.

Teachers and parents can use this book to help children identify their behavior at each of the five stages and remember things they can do if their worries get too big. The book opens with Nicholas, who talks about how children with anxiety and behavior problems can be very intelligent and do things well. He asks the readers to identify what they do well in a drawing or in writing. Nicholas then introduces the first stage, "1," explaining that a "1" feeling is one of relaxation and enjoyment. He also identifies things that help people who worry feel they are at a "1," such as being reassured by knowing what will happen next. Nicholas then works readers through the various stages and asks them to indicate in illustrations and/or writing what makes them feel as if they are at a "5." He introduces several strategies that children and youth can use to get back to a "1" and asks them to draw and identify their own relaxation strategies. This exercise helps turn the abstract concept of tantrums, and meltdowns into something concrete and personal. Teachers and parents, by reading the book with children, help them understand their behavior and its cause.

To add to the tremendous benefits of this book, a 5-point thermometer is introduced at the end that the teacher and child can complete to identify behaviors at each stage and what the child can do to help himself feel like his worrying is at a "1." This simple thermometer is brilliant. It places on one small piece of paper everything about the "bigness of her worries" for a particular child. The child can have the thermometer on her desk or velcroed inside her textbook or notebook for easy reference throughout the day.

The applicability of this strategy is broad. I envision a child who has used Kari's book in a general education class. He has a thermometer on his desk and the teacher carries a duplicate on the back of her school I.D. badge. When she looks to the child periodically, she discreetly turns her badge around to silently ask the child how big his worry is. He points to his thermometer in response; they smile knowingly at each other. Finally, to go along with the 5-point thermometer, the author has developed a helpful Stress Scale and accompanying calming sequence that can be individualized for each child.

When My Worries Get Too Big! is a wonderful book. It is a simple-to-use strategy that can help children and youth be successful. Children who use this book will find themselves relaxed and ready to work or play. In Kari's words, children with anxiety and emotional regulation difficulties will realize that "They are awesome and in control!"

Thank you, Kari, for this brilliant and easy-to-use intervention!

— Brenda Smith Myles, PhD

Dear Parents and Teachers,

Anxiety is a normal reaction to stress and can actually be beneficial in some situations. However, problems arise when anxiety becomes excessive and disabling - interfering with typical daily activities at home and at school, including how children learn, behave, and cope with their emotions.

Heightened levels of anxiety are increasingly common among children. In fact, anxiety disorders are the most frequent of all mental disorders in children. According to the Centers for Disease Control and Prevention (CDC), approximately 4.4 million children in the United States have diagnosed anxiety.

More than any other issue for children with anxiety, loss of emotional control can lead to removal from the general education classroom to a more restrictive educational environment equipped to deal with behavior challenges. Sometimes this means a special room at school; sometimes it means a special program outside of the neighborhood school.

Even when children are able to stay in the general education classroom, watching a child lose control of her emotions is scary, and peers are likely to avoid a child who "explodes" without warning. Therefore, it is critical that we help children with anxiety learn to understand and control their emotions. This is an important reminder because those of us who teach and live with children who are anxious are often so focused on teaching them other things that we forget that teaching someone to relax can benefit them in life more than any skill or academic content.

A loss of emotional control can hinder a child's social success from a very young age. The following is a wonderfully heartfelt example of this written by a man with Tourette Syndrome about his own early signs of explosive anxiety.

> Adam, with his large sky-blue eyes, rosy cheeks, and curly hair should be an irresistible two and a half year old. When the sweet, elderly woman in the supermarket pats him on the head, and tries to engage his attention, he lets out a bloodcurdling shriek. He nearly throws himself

out of the shopping cart. This kindly senior citizen has just disrupted his tally of grocery products that begin with the letter "B." He needed to remember them in the exact order in which his shopping cart passed them. He is now in aisle thirteen! He screams, inconsolable, because he knows that his mother will not walk up and down each and every aisle letting him recheck his list.

Adam's mother isn't necessarily unreasonable. She just can't figure out why her child is screaming, because Adam still can't talk. What his mother doesn't yet know is that her son has been reading since he was a little more than a year old. There is a method to his madness that she can't even imagine. She is embarrassed and confused. The unsuspecting elderly woman no longer finds him at all appealing.
(Adam DePrince, 1992, p. 21)

This book was originally written for a kindergarten student who had difficulty tolerating the everyday surprises that school offers, such as when the daily schedule was interrupted to fit in a school assembly or when a substitute teacher came for the day. Originally, I taught this student a relaxation routine we called "Relaxed Body" — a routine inspired by my friend Joyce Santo, who had been teaching her four- and five-year-old autistic students to complete a relaxation routine prior to stressful events.

"Relaxed Body" went something like this:
1. Take three long breaths.
2. Stretch your arms up over your head, down and up again.
3. Rub your hands together and count to 3.
4. Rub your thighs and count to 3.
5. Take another long breath.

My experience with this student impressed upon me that a highly anxious five-year-old was capable of learning the first steps to relaxation.

It is important for parents and teachers to realize that anxiety is very real. Even if the child's fear or worry seems unreasonable to you, it should never just be dismissed. It is also important to remember that "worry thoughts" reach the brain before "thinking thoughts." One way to keep the initial worry thoughts from getting too big, therefore, is to learn a predictable, overlearned routine so that when the worry hits, the child can go through the routine without thinking, kind of like how we use the 911 routine to help us remember how to access help, even when we are faced with a crisis.

Another important point to remember is that explosive behavior is personal. Losing control is embarrassing for the child, and even if remorse is not clear to you, the act of losing control can cause great concern for the child. As a result, the child is likely to become resistant to discussing his behavior, for fear it is a character flaw and that there might be something seriously wrong with him. When this happens, parents and teachers need to make their suggestions for change as nonconfrontational as possible.

This book gives children the opportunity to label and define their own levels 1-5 and share how each level feels on their personalized Stress Scale. Refer to the back of the book for more ideas about how to work with anxious children.

This is not a quick fix, and teaching relaxation is a long process, but the long-term benefits are well worth the effort. I hope you find this book useful in the process

-Kari

Sometimes kids have worries but they also have things they are really good at.

I am really good at

_____

_____

_____

Here I am doing my favorite thing.

When I am thinking about my favorite things, I am so relaxed. My worries are at a 1 or 2.

When I know what is going to happen or I really like what I am doing, I am most definitely at a **1** or **2**.

But sometimes I worry too much, like when I first get on the bus and I don't know where to sit.

...but I don't know where to sit!

When I worry too much,
my worries are at a 4.
Sometimes a **4** makes
my stomach hurt.

Sometimes I worry way too much, like when I think I am going to recess and it gets canceled!

This might make me scream or even hit someone. This is a **5**. Now my worries are TOO BIG!

One thing that makes my worries too big is

_____

_____

_____

Here I am at a ⑤

This is when I need
to fight back!
First, I can squeeze my
hands together.

Next, I can take three really slow, deep breaths. Slow in – slow out, slow in – slow out, slow in – slow out.

Then I can sit down, rub my legs and close my eyes. Now I feel more like a **3** or a **2**.

I can think about happy things, like my dog or my stuffed lion, or our family cabin in the summer. Now I am at a 1.

Here are some things that I can think about to help me bring a 5 feeling down to a 1 feeling.

You can do other things
to help you relax.
You can go for a walk,
go to your bedroom, or go
to a safe place at school.

Here I am relaxed and ready to work.
I am at a 1, feeling good and feeling proud!

Let me tell you about my worries
(Write about how they look.
Write about how they
make your body feel.)

5

4

3

2

1

Fill in Your Own Stress Scale

Level	Person, place or thing	Makes me feel like this:
5		This could make me lose control!!!!
4		This can really upset me.
3		This can make me feel nervous.
2		This bothers me a little.
1		This never bothers me.

Now think of 2 things you can do at each level to make things better.

Level	Person, place or thing	Makes me feel like this:	I can try to do this:
5		This could make me lose control!!!!	
4		This can really upset me.	
3		This can make me feel nervous.	
2		This bothers me a little.	
1		This never bothers me.	

My Calming Sequence

Sometimes my worries are way too big! I can stop, squeeze my hands, and take a deep breath. I can also rub my head and rub my legs. This can help me to stay calm.

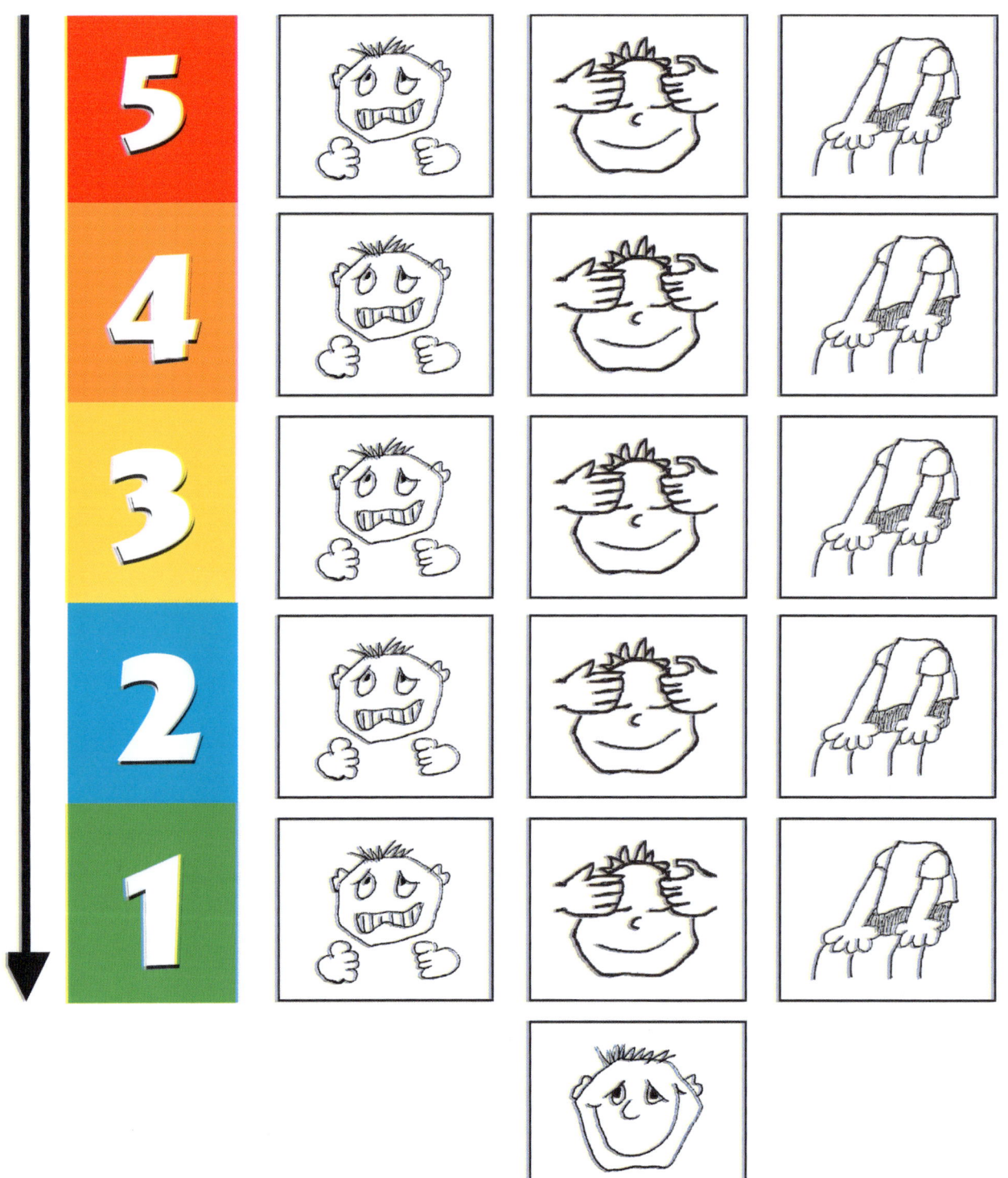

Kari Dunn Buron, Sandra Manns, Lynette Schultz and Shelly Thomas

My Calming Sequence

(The following two visual supports may be photocopied and laminated to be carried in a backpack, pocket or purse for handy reference.)

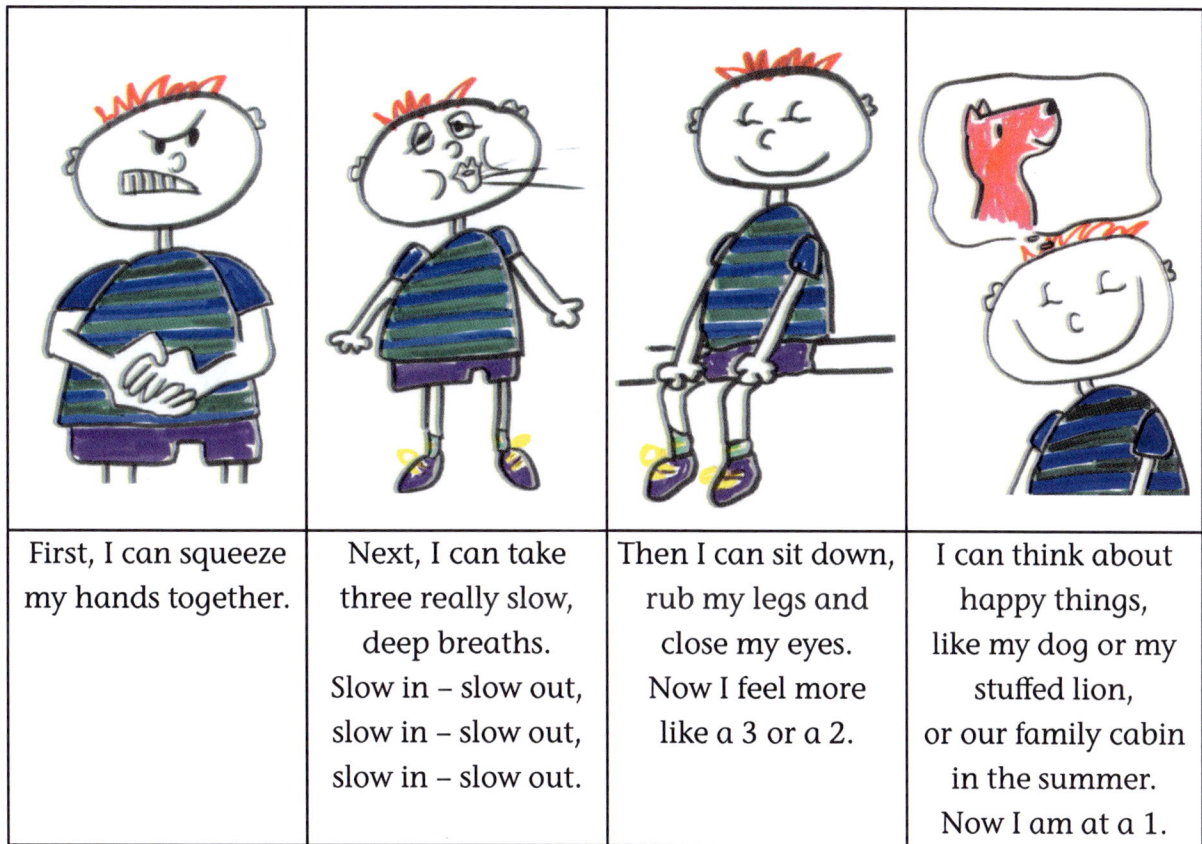

First, I can squeeze my hands together.	Next, I can take three really slow, deep breaths. Slow in – slow out, slow in – slow out, slow in – slow out.	Then I can sit down, rub my legs and close my eyes. Now I feel more like a 3 or a 2.	I can think about happy things, like my dog or my stuffed lion, or our family cabin in the summer. Now I am at a 1.

Suggested Calming Strategy

1. Take three long breaths.
2. Stretch your arms up over your head, down and up again.
3. Rub your hands together and count to 3.
4. Rub your thighs and count to 3.
5. Take another long breath.

Using When My Worries Get Too Big in a Therapy Setting

When My Worries Get Too Big is a wonderful resource for children, and for people in general, who experience anxiety. I have used it, and The Incredible 5-Point Scale for individuals of all ages in both the school and the therapy setting. I have most often seen these two resources in the school setting but have used them effectively in my own therapy practice for many years and now utilize them when training other clinicians to work with autistic clients (NOTE: As a neurodiversity affirming therapist, I use identity first language intentionally).

As a therapist working with autistic clients who present with symptoms that may be indicative of a diagnosis other than autism, the 5-Point Scale lends itself well to individualization. For those who are not yet in touch with their feelings, adding a column to describe what an emotion "feels like" is often helpful. In therapy, we almost always add a column for "What I Can Do". It has been a privilege to be able to guide clients as they learn about their anxious feelings, how those feelings grow, and what to do about them. This journey nearly always begins with the story of When My Worries Get Too Big! Children enjoy the story. Sometimes we make a chart showing how they are the same or different from the child in the story. Parents, while they are in the waiting area, are given a copy of the book and find Kari's explanations to be quite helpful.

When working with teens we often talk about how to "upgrade" the story. I typically explain that the ideas in the story are well known to most adults, and that managing anxiety is a part of adult life. I tell them that this story is helpful for children who need to learn about managing their emotions. I invite them to make changes in the story so it fits teens. In most cases, this turns out to be an engaging activity that we are able to do together. Along the way, these teens become better at identifying and managing their own anxiety.

Judy Endow, LCSW[*]
Author and International Speaker

---

[*] Judy was the first autistic person to receive the *Autism Society of America's Cathy Pratt Professional of the Year Award*

Recommendations for Teachers and Parents

Understanding the nature of anxiety is extremely important. A loss of emotional control can negatively impact a child's success with all relationships throughout all environments. For example, if a child experiences anxiety at a birthday party due to some unforeseen event, the anxious feeling may lead to a loss of emotional control, resulting in negative or scary behavior. This unexpected behavior, when witnessed by the other children, may lead to social rejection.

Adults often respond to a child's aggressive behavior by using motivational systems such as sticker charts or losing privileges. Using these motivational methods assumes the child already has the skills needed to change, and that he would change if he just wanted to badly enough. When a child has such high levels of stress and anxiety that he totally loses control, it is helpful for all caregivers to rethink how they are thinking about the resulting behavior (Greene, 1998). For example, Greene reminds us that:

- Tantrum behavior is typically seen in 2-year-olds.
- Two-year olds have tantrums because developmentally they do not have good emotional regulation skills.
- When a child lacks skills beyond the developmentally expected age, the result may be considered a learning disability.
- Having frequent tantrums beyond the toddler years can be considered a developmental learning disability – the inability to manage or control one's emotions.
- Learning disabilities require adaptive teaching, beyond and different from what might be typically used. The following are some strategies you can try when working with or parenting a child with anxiety who lacks emotional regulation skills.

After reading this book with a child, you can expand on the scale idea by talking to her about her feelings in terms of numbers. You can help her sort out the difference between just being excited because something is fun (being at a 3) and falling into the 4 range, where she may be so excited that she is almost losing control. Another example of expanding on the idea might be to talk about big problems and little problems and problems that are in between. An anxious child might think that any problem is a major obstacle and therefore over-react. The scale can help a child visualize and comprehend the difference between little problems, problems that are irritating, problems that are inconvenient, problems that make him mad, and problems that will change his life!

The calming routine presented in this story can be made into a poster to use as a teaching tool for the child. A small prompt card with a picture of the sequence can then be used to visually prompt the child to start his calming sequence* in predictably stressful settings. For example, if the child tends to get upset when it is time to leave the park, you can show him the small prompt card to remind him to take deep breaths, etc. to help calm his body and make it easier to accept the bad news about leaving.

---

*   The calming sequence can be downloaded from my website www.5pointscale.com.

Evidence-Based Strategies for Proactively Supporting Highly Anxious Children

1. Create a Pensieve

In the *Harry Potter* series (J. K. Rowling), there is a very wise wizard named Albus Dumbledore. Dumbledore has a tremendous amount of responsibility and knows a lot of things. Sometimes he gets overwhelmed with thoughts and memories, so he puts them into a shallow stone basin called a pensieve.

Using this strategy is in line with the evidence-based practice of self-management (National Autism Center, 2015) as it teaches the child to put some worries on the back burner until he has time to work it out.

Start by making a pensieve out of a small shoebox for the highly anxious child you live or are working with. Make a slot in the top and have the child decorate the outside. On 3x5 note cards, have the child write down worrisome thoughts, with your assistance as needed. Prompt the child to put the cards into the pensieve and let him know that you will revisit them later when you can help him work on one worry at a time.

2. Establish a Worry Place

Adults often use the strategy of timeout (TO) in rather punitive ways. We connect timeout places with statements like, "because you did X, you need to take a timeout." Even though taking a break away from a difficult situation can be very effective for everyone, children quickly connect TO with a negative place.

In order to turn this around, try establishing a worry place. This is a place a child can go to where she does not have to talk or answer questions. This is a calm spot, possibly equipped with paper and drawing materials, photo albums, jigsaw puzzles, or soft snuggly items. In the children's chapter book Adalyn's Clare (Buron, 2021), the main character uses a popup tent as her worry place. Teaching a child to use a worry place is a form of self-management, which is an evidence-based practice (National Autism Center, 2015).

3. Using Photographs to Teach Imagery

The concept of imagery can be difficult for young children to understand because it involves making a shift from a negative thought to a positive thought by imagining something positive in their heads.

Photos can be used to assist children in "conjuring up" such positive images. It is also helpful to use concrete language when working with children, such as "replace the worry thought" and "find the calming thought" rather than "imagine" that ....

I recommend the use of a small photo album with photos of things the child loves. Focus on the things that tend to be calming (family pet, child's bed, stuffed animal, a family vacation or the child participating in a calming activity like swimming) rather than things that tend to be alerting (video games or other types of games, TV programs, etc.). As the child looks at the photos depicting known positive events, he is encouraged simultaneously to take slow, deep breaths. This is a type of relaxation and a form of teaching self-management, which is an evidence-based practice (National Autism Center, 2015).

4. Make "Rules" Into "Guidelines for Success"

Teachers and parents often rely of "rules" to maintain some sense of order at home or at school. Such rules help to structure the environment and set boundaries and, ultimately, benefit everybody. However, children who experience excessive anxiety have most likely had quite a few "run-ins" with the adult authority figures, who establish and implement these rules, including you. Sometimes this leads to either rigid adherence to rules or rejecting rules altogether.

One idea to help prevent such situations is to change the terminology used from "rules" to "guidelines." Such an apparently slight change actually takes the pressure off (pressure typically increases anxiety!) and, therefore, lessens the chance of overly rigid behavior. Try posting a list of Guidelines for Social Success and ask everybody to follow them. Using this new terminology, if the child makes a social blunder (like yelling out a swear word in class or insulting somebody), rather than having committed the apparently more serious offense of "breaking the rules," it means that she simply has not followed the guidelines, and consequently will probably not be very socially successful. This approach makes use of an antecedent package, an evidence-based practice, by modifying the environment (through change in terminology) in anticipation of a problem (resistance to "rules") (National Autism Center, 2015).

5. Use a Calendar to Add Structure

Organization is very calming, and using schedules and other visual systems as a way to organize the day, the environment, etc., is supported in the evidence-based practice literature (The National Professional Development Center on Autism Spectrum Disorders, 2014). When we know ahead of time what is going on, what is happening when, or if a planned event has been changed or canceled, it helps us to feel in control and, therefore, calmer.

One very simple way to add a sense of structure to life is to put up a calendar either in

> Some calendars designed for classrooms merely teach the date without noting any events or changes. This design is not as helpful if teaching organizational skills.

your home or your classroom. The calendar should be functional, with plenty of room on each day to write any information about events. Teach the child to check the calendar every day to keep track of (a) changes in the typical schedule, (b) special occasions like birthdays, (c) a parent out of town, etc.

6. Take an Adult Timeout

For years I was told to address negative behavior immediately. This led to confronting highly anxious children when they were still in the throes of anxiety, and rather then helping, my behavior actually made the situation worse by creating more stress in an already stressful situation. In addition, the increased stress made it harder for the child to make a good choice as anxiety decreases a person's ability to think, learn or process information effectively.

Try to break the habit of responding immediately by staying calm and quiet. This approach makes use of an antecedent package, an evidence-based practice, by modifying staff or adult behavior (National Autism Center, 2015). You can process negative behavior later when everyone is calm. Generally, a calm child is a more receptive child.

References

Buron, K.D (2021). Adalyn 's Clare. Saint Paul, MN: 5 Point Scale Publishing. www.5pointscale.com

DePrince, A. (1992). Tourette Syndrome: Uncute and Unendearing. In J. Hilkevich & A. Seligman (Eds). Don't Think About Monkeys. P.21. Durante, CA: Hope Press.

Greene, R. (1998). The Explosive Child. New York, NY: Harper Collins.

The National Autism Center (2015). Evidence-based practice and autism in the schools: A guide to providing appropriate interventions to students with autism spectrum disorders.

The National Professional Development Center on Autism Spectrum Disorders. (2014). Evidence based practice briefs.

About the Author

Kari Dunn Buron taught autistic students in K-12 in Minnesota for 30+ years and was a founding member of the Minnesota Autism Project. She developed the Autism Certificate program for educators at Hamline University in St. Paul, MN, and has done volunteer work specific to autism in Trinidad and Tobago, Barbados, Tanzania, Ghana, Nigeria, and Nepal. In 2003, Kari received a Leadership Fellowship that allowed her to complete a self-designed study of the links between social cognition, explosive behavior, education and autism. In 2012, Kari was inducted into the Illinois State University Education Department Hall of Fame.

Kari is the co-author of multiple books for educators including The Incredible 5-Point Scale, Social Behavior and Self-Management, and the author of A 5 Could Make Me Lose Control and A 5 is Against the Law! She is the author of Adalyn's Clare, a story about a highly anxious 4th grader who has difficulty with emotional control. Kari is currently writing Adalyn's Clare as a screen play, and continues to self-publish her work through 5 Point Scale Publishing.

5 Point Scale Publishing
www.5pointscale.com

Printed in Great Britain
by Amazon